TO LITERALLY YOU

PAUL KILLEBREW

CANARIUM BOOKS
ANN ARBOR, MARFA, IOWA CITY

SPONSORED BY
THE HELEN ZELL WRITERS' PROGRAM
AT THE UNIVERSITY OF MICHIGAN

TO LITERALLY YOU

Canarium Books
Ann Arbor, Marfa, Iowa City
www.canarium.org

The editors gratefully acknowledge the
Helen Zell Writers' Program at the University of Michigan
for editorial assistance and generous support.

Cover: Martha E. Hughes, *Centimeter 22*.
Prismacolor on paper, 2012.
Used courtesy of the artist.

Design: Gou Dao Niao

First Edition

Printed in the United States of America

ISBN 13: 978-0-9969827-4-0

CONTENTS

COMMON POINTLESS   1

ELEGY FOR 39   9

37TH BIRTHDAY ELEGY FOR TRAVIS   13

DAD AT 63   19

CRYING DEAD LIGHTS   26

NOON KNOWLEDGE   34

ACTUALLY PRESENT   42

THOSE FEELINGS OF COMPLETE DESPERATION   43

JEAN DUBUFFET JOHN WIENERS SHAWN KILLEBREW   49

ANYONE'S TWO MINUTES   60

TO LITERALLY YOU   62

WHAT I TOOK TO BE RESIGNATION   68

ACKNOWLEDGMENTS   83

COMMON POINTLESS

I wonder if I've really scrutinized this experience like
you're supposed to have if you can type

— Frank O'Hara, "For the Chinese New Year & for Bill Berkson"

I was born in Tennessee.
I was raised on ideas.
Now I fall down
as a person
in bodily emulsion.
But spiritually speaking?
I'm not suffering.
I'm looking at nine pictures on a light blue wall
in black frames with white matting.
In one the Secretary of Defense walks through Iraq
in a suit and boots,
surrounded by a thick white line.
If it wasn't like this I wouldn't care,
which is not to say I wouldn't mind.
Some find this layering of thoughts
within the ever-diminishing moment
to be a complete defense to the charge of privilege,
but surely more is expected, and there is no defense;
we commit crimes
and show ourselves and each other
unbelievable mercy.
To be meticulous is to give up in a way still marked by effort,
which for many is the one, true art.
What did the New Critics think about plagiarism?

Repetition as a form of time travel?
Conservatives prefer repetition in service
of an incantatory mourning for a lost world,
but one plagiarizes the self
in the commission of boredom.
Maybe it's the difference between new meanings
and a complex weave of old ones,
or those who hold no new meanings are possible.
Or maybe all that's possible
is a new ordering of priorities within experiences.
A sensibility and its chosen course are what matter most to me.
The present calcifies into interlocking crystals,
leaving so much gratuitous precedent
to be lined up in the narrow hallway of one's attention
that a trajectory could be plotted to anywhere.
You go through each room and remove a single wall,
but only in your mind,
and still the house collapses. It wasn't built to last.
What kind of imposition would that have been anyway?
Words on a page
and a bare molecule of intentionality
coming through this pinhole of sensation and time.
My face, lit by screens
and angled penitently towards coffee,
withers like a democracy
under its loudest features.
Sometimes it's hard to watch,
I know. Not at all like yours, or yours,
presences to which my life
is a distracted vigil,

having found no higher calling.
Certainly not this,
which could happen or not
and all that's at stake
is whether I've told you.
You drive us through the rain in Virginia
after taking me to see
my 93-year-old grandfather in Nashville.
My dad and I went to his hospital room at night,
where he told me about the Korean man
he'd met at the church he built in Nagoya
who had to hide from police
after becoming a suspect in the kidnapping of a local teenager.
He hadn't kidnapped her.
Years later they learned
she'd run away in the middle of the night
to avoid an arranged marriage.
But prejudice against Koreans
ran high in late forties Japan,
so my grandfather's friend became the target
of an investigation whose misguidedness
ensured its longevity.
I forgot to ask my grandfather, whose name is Ernest,
what Nagoya was like in the late forties,
after a quarter of the city was incinerated
by American firebombing
that Robert McNamara, who also lived to see 93,
later conceded was a war crime.
A few weeks after the Korean man disappeared
he called Ernest and asked to meet

at a popular restaurant in town.
Ernest arrived at the appointed time
and found the restaurant packed with people.
A hostess, upon learning whom Ernest was meeting,
directed him to the restaurant's second floor,
which he found completely empty
except for his friend
who sat alone at a table at the far end
and waved Ernest over
as soon as he came up the stairs.
They talked for a couple of hours,
during which time the man explained
that he was innocent,
but, given the conditions in Nagoya,
he would have to remain out of sight,
at least for now.
He thanked Ernest for his friendship
and went on to explain
that he owned the restaurant they were sitting in,
as well as a couple of nearby hotels,
and he was actually quite wealthy.
A few years later,
Ernest's job as a missionary
was moving him to Tokyo,
and apparently his friend learned he was leaving
because he called Ernest again
and asked to meet at ten the next night,
this time at an address my grandfather recognized
as being in the industrial section of town,
mainly warehouses and the like,

with few stores or restaurants
and probably no people around so late.
With some trepidation,
Ernest went to the address at ten
and waited. The streets were empty
except, after fifteen or twenty minutes,
a yakimo man whom Ernest heard a couple of blocks away.
Yakimo men drive carts around at night
selling sweet potatoes—yakimo—that are roasted over charcoal
on the cart itself. You can hear them at night bellowing out,
"Yaaakiiiiiiiiiiiiimooooooo!" Eventually the yakimo man
came right up next to Ernest, then stopped his cart
and said, in Japanese, "It's me."
It was his friend,
who explained that this was one
of several disguises
his circumstances unfortunately required.
He said he'd heard Ernest would soon be moving,
and he just wanted to see him again
to thank him for his friendship.
They spoke briefly,
and then my grandfather's friend rolled his cart away,
occasionally calling out, "Yaaakiiiiiiiiiiiiimooooooo!"
And now you and I
are driving through Virginia again,
the sky a further gray.
I woke up this morning with you
in Roanoke, thirty-five years old
for the first time, in love
and astonished. I jogged three miles

while listening to "The Weight" seven times in a row
and thought the song
could be a pacifist anthem:
you righteous people
go on and kill each other;
all us sinners will be here,
living in peace and mutual assistance.
The feeling vanished, or perhaps deepened
past visibility, when I heard about the acquittal. Bastille Day.
A wary sun bided its time
in the drowsy grad school of an overcast sky,
and then, finding its moment,
delivered a bleaching intensity
to the reading glasses
resting on the dashboard
of our financed Acura
under a dewy windshield,
casting bleary water shadows
through the double lens
of windshield and glasses
across the car's front seat,
the deep blue fabric of which
was brushed into dark and light patches
working crossways from the sun
cast complexly through fat leaves
of the adjoining yard's many hardwoods.
A single leaf shadow
bobbled over the plastic lid
of a day-old coffee cup
sitting in the center console

next to the gear shift,
white and blue-gray
mixing over the still black hole of the spout,
a small, circular cinema.
Doubled, tiny threads of dust on the rearview
glowed in a stripe of light
reflected from the trunk forward,
trembling minutely
as the air inside the Acura
warmed, circulated, and gained humidity,
seashells of fog
developing from the bottom of the windshield
at the defroster's vents.
Spots of dew on the roof
shrank as they dried,
leaving concentric trails of pollen and air dirt
in a yellow-brown haze
against the car's light blue exterior,
sediment at the level of microns
building glacially over weeks
of quickly warming summer mornings.
Seatbelts and downward seams in the upholstery
lent no sense of vertical logic to the interior.
The passenger side buckle rested partially
on a pile of folders and papers in the seat.
The silver tip of the buckle
breached the edge of a pie chart
printed on the piece of paper
at the top of the pile.
The chart was in grayscale

and demonstrated striking productivity.
Before the dewdrops on the windshield dried,
the bumpy shadows of four of them
fell evenly along the rounded edge
of the chart's largest triangle,
giving the edge's black line
the appearance of growing darker
as it travelled through the dewdrop shadows.
Up very close, the paper itself
was a thicket of rough fibers,
a cotton ball flattened,
and the black line of the chart's edge
was a dense, black dust
resting on the thicket,
containing to one side
a far less concentrated
swarm of black particles.

ELEGY FOR 39

It was the year we decided not
to get divorced. The poem
said something like clouds
moving quickly across the sun
while the rest of us talked about faith
and how my personal level of intensity
in faking it is one way to measure
the depth of the drop I'd have to make
before I could turn over in bed
toward a window open to the night
and spotty rain dotting leaves
with light caught from porch lamps
and know that what I'd imagined
to be time drained of sound
was the purest sound,
one person turning away from another
into a cone formed by his turning.
We sat on the porch while the kids napped
and watched light rise and fall
through clouds moving quickly across the sun
like distractions from a vital and complex truth
that requires too many pages of exegesis
for people with days like ours,
time's version of an optical illusion,
both too long and too short
for anything like actual thinking.
I remember one of the many unsolicited
pieces of advice we got when Elmer
was coming along—don't make any major

decisions until he's one, you'll be too
tired to get it right. So naturally
we changed jobs and moved across the country.
I can't even remember who gave us that advice.
They're probably out of our lives now.
And what's in them, these six and something
years out of your forty and my almost
that we've been spinning through together,
watching our obligations mount
around sensations that folded out of us
from zones of our beings we hadn't
seen before, like a third arm you'd
somehow failed to notice, an us
both alien and uncannily us,
children, a marriage, an unexpected love—
these things have taken over,
brushed aside whatever
was there before
like an anxious developer.
This force is of
our own making but comically
has no regard for us, like that arm
is a whole body, two bodies,
tugging us along wherever they feel like going,
the most dangerous places they can find.
I was writing that line on my phone
while following fifteen-month-old Harlan
doing his duck walk down a wheelchair ramp.
He leaned way over the side of it
to look at some smooth rocks on the ground

and, as I got to the word "dangerous,"
toppled down into them.
So much for art, some might say,
but not me, I just learned
how many people have put videos online
with the words "spectacular sunset" in their titles,
there's one after another.
I'd made one myself, a video I mean,
because the sun had ducked
behind an unmoving cloud
at the horizon, and I knew from the internet
how long it would take the sun to reappear
in the gap between the bottom edge of the cloud
and the top edge of the earth,
a sun-sized gap dotted with its own
minor cloud variants
there to complicate the image,
a sun moving slowly behind clouds,
and I felt a low note being struck within,
something I've learned is not sadness
but gratitude in unknowing,
a feeling that is hard but porous,
that dissipates like short rain
steaming off its first idea of the ground.
Dark pink reformatting the blue,
dark pink lights of our forever car,
dark pink of hippies, dark pink life tassels,
dark pink "to fly," as you put it,
"by the night of our pants."
I don't know where the night goes,

but I know we'll be awake,
and why, this long year of nights
when people standing right next to us
broke in half and spilled everywhere
just because they paid attention.
We don't have an exact date
for when we got engaged,
there was no moment, no single question
but instead weeks of them
while an idea changed from something we could do
into something we would, it was gestational,
like this year has been, a year I hope is over.
I'm glad you're turning forty. I wish I were, too.
I need a number for what we've come through,
our second engagement, longer than the first,
permanent, in fact, the questions of questions
and the answer we give—
give, deny, and give again.

37TH BIRTHDAY ELEGY FOR TRAVIS

If one train leaves your childhood,
is what I thought on the street
of wide-wale driveways, colorless
blue houses, and collages
of the uncontemplative glance
toward what was either the sound
of a person in sudden pain
or the arrival of light within
the pure spherical sensation
of presence, the arrival of light
in the geometry's spaces broken
into ideas. I was thinking like a test:
If one train leaves your infancy,
will it arrive at adulthood
at the same time
the train leaving your childhood
arrives at your 37th birthday?
On my own 37th, I struggled to think
of anything that made it anything
more than a house
among similar others, significant
perhaps for its houseness but not
otherwise worth pointing out,
just a corner you stood on
waiting for one light to turn off
and another to turn on,
but the calculation did seem like something,
maybe, that 37 is 18 times 2 plus 1,
that I had then been alive in my

obligations longer than I had been
exempt from true regret, and while
I can often be observed
reaching past the sufficient
for the provocative belief,
I did feel an older kind of older,
of another order, mathematically
more adult than child. I remember
in my college evangelical days
trying to convince you that God
would roll up a life's experience
like a sheet of paper and look through it,
and I remember forgetting this,
or at least it never occurring to me,
until you brought it up a few years ago
when Maggie and I were in Chicago
to meet Malcolm at eleven weeks
before Elmer, who wasn't yet Elmer,
was born, two more trains
departing from us now for something else
unknowable and utterly unexplainable
to them in their minds that dilate
like a flower exploding into confetti,
and we could probably calculate the date
that's either recently past or coming up soon
when we will have known each other
longer than we haven't, which was what
the story of the life tube
brought to my mind just now,
that if the God that is the culmination

of all suffering were looking for patterns,
I might request its indulgence
for just a moment as I flatten out
the sheet of paper on which my notes
are written and find the single verb
that appears within them
across all permutations of tense,
a word I sense must be there
but could not even guess what it is
until I look, or you tell me.
That wasn't part of the story
I told when I was nineteen.
I assume without examining
the question too closely
that I remember almost nothing
about that person,
the person I am in every literal
but no figurative sense.
I feel you rising already
to contest that statement.
You'd know better than me,
that's what knowing someone
for so long means, if
the accumulation of time
in the presence of another
means anything at all,
or if instead the natural world
remains in equipoise
no matter how many ideas
we could ever think about it.

How comical, then, to write them down
and expect anything to happen,
though, and I'm sure we've
discussed this all before,
the nothing that can be called upon
may be preferable anyway,
or anyway we continue to write,
that's what we had in common
to begin with, not that it was so
exotic or certainly any good.
I often find the accuracy of my own
feelings of inadequacy to be oddly
reassuring, though I know—this
is my point—how that must sound.
Don't you think it's fair to start
drawing a few conclusions,
that the piling up of life behind us
is beginning to be a little
daunting? Or are these only
the colors of the houses,
the temporary and unplaceable sounds
common to this part of the neighborhood,
a weather of the senses
that one shouldn't confuse
with a more permanent desire?
On my current commute
I pass a statue of Abraham Lincoln,
standing, life-sized, right hand
either dropping or picking up
a sheaf of invisible papers,

inexplicably placed outside the DC
Court of Appeals, where it's hard
for me to imagine what business
an Illinois lawyer may have had,
though there is an inscription
that I haven't bothered to stop to read
even once among the hundreds of times
I've passed it, but it's at the moment
each morning that I do,
the moment when I pass by Lincoln's feet,
that the Washington Monument appears
from behind an ugly apartment building,
structures from which Lincoln himself
is turned away. I couldn't remember today
where on my walk I was supposed
to see the Washington Monument,
and it seemed briefly possible
that it was gone. Then it wasn't.
I liked it better when it was covered
in scaffolding, as the capitol dome is now.
If the scaffolding were permanent,
it might remind us where we are
with regard to the damage of the past,
or, if these grand impositions
would just disappear occasionally,
the possibility of renewal.
But the work of persisting
seems to go on without interruption,
a single track slowly falling
farther out of the sky

to an earth we once inhabited
at the fringes of personhood,
the patio where we met
half these lifetimes ago and decided
at some level of ourselves
to leave.

DAD AT 63

I thought about the first lines
of *The Making of Americans*:

> Once an angry man
> dragged his father along the ground
> through his own orchard. "Stop!"
> cried the groaning old man at last,
> "Stop! I did not drag my father
> beyond this tree."

Robert Creeley paraphrased this parable
in a poem to his son, Will,
with whom I went (of all places) to law school.
I wonder what sense
Gertrude Stein intended,
inheritance as limit, the edges of definition?
And memory. Mine is being rewritten
by parenting and divorce, a vortex
of formation and destruction.
"Already we'd come a long distance together,"
Creeley wrote. "It was time now
for something other." Criminal
to break his line. Criminal to paraphrase
Stein. And yet some things were the same.
I strapped Harlan into his high chair
and gave him what soon became a handful
of sandwich. That was in the past.
But the relative present. I thought
"to past" would make a nice verb,
transitive, to transmit something
from this temporal sphere to the previous—

morning pasts night, having children
pasts youth, birthdays past ages,
divorce pasts marriage.
Maybe it only begs to define
the full reach of the present.
Your sixtieth birthday is in the past.
We sat in our yard at the long, yellow table
splotched white by sunlight
warbling through leaves,
a scattering of newspaper
and stuff from the sandwich place,
Shawn's family, all of them,
staying with us, you and mom at a hotel,
and the night before with the cake I made,
narrow wedges of chocolate,
kids crowded around the candle.
I thought you were distant
within normal vectors and besides
I'd never turned sixty or lost
a dad at sixty-one. It's different
in the revision. I think of you thinking
What the hell am I doing,
asking mom too carefully in the morning
if she's ready to go, sitting among us
in our far-off approximations
suspended by the contrail of events
you'd not yet granted us the eyes to see.
You were, in this way, in the separate room
you've wanted and had for most of your life.
Left alone there. In the painting you made

of our wedding, most figures are separate
chapters. The painting's two pairings
are uncomfortable, mom refusing
to face Lynn directly—a celebrity
to paparazzi—while Maggie and I celebrate
by a tree, alone. At our wedding.
Twenty people in the painting
and none of them look directly
at anyone else. I told you
it was like an Altman movie,
the assaultive presence of others,
Adam Sandler at dinner with his sisters
in *Punch Drunk Love*. By which I mean,
I get it. Marriage is an unreliable narrator.
The self in its messiness calls for
various forms. The plot in James Salter's
Light Years proceeds by openings—
new characters, new settings
introduced every few pages,
with the tedium of
narrative connection among them
left oblique or unresolved.
It made me want to write a novel
that would be a series of thresholds,
each chapter only the beginning
of a chapter. That's how it feels
sometimes, striding down
this narrative trajectory.
There is a sense, too, that irresolution
collects in the atmosphere,

that its morality is accretive.
At what point will your marriage
be in the past? Its erasure
is smeared across years. Like paint.
To paint this would have been
better, to put it in your orchard
rather than mine, though I think
of the orchard in Stein as a stand-in
for lineage, like citation. But citation
is voluntary. Inheritance is something
that happens to you, the comedy of recognition,
the tragedy. The man who drags his father
along the ground through an orchard
believes his act is his own. But it's
a replica. Like clones who don't know
they're clones. You have two sons,
I have two sons. We all feel loved.
Salter exalts the love of the parent
as "the true love," writes that while
romantic love "was what life was seeking;
it was a suspension of life," loving a child
"for whom one spent everything,
whose life was protected and nourished
by one's own, to have that child beside one,
at peace, was the real, the deepest,
the only joy." Distinctions.
To invest dissimilar things
with an aura of deep connection
might be an act of metaphor
but also marketing. To go the other way,

then. Having children is an immersion.
Having parents is different.
I can't tell who my kids look like,
all I see is them. But yesterday
I noticed my shoes in a recent photo
and the way my ankles locked into them,
the shoes low and simple, beat-up,
white soles heavily bruised,
the ankles thin and mechanical—
these were things I'd seen before.
You had us young so I don't know
if this was the same for you,
but by the time we got married and pregnant
Maggie and I had narrowed to a wire
the size of the words we sent
back home to do in the place
of true familiarity. And with,
we both believed, good reason.
We were formed by absences,
by the abstraction of previous selves
and the disasters of everyone's
specious bullshit they morphed
to absorb or deflect. Differentiation.
To locate and name the derivative.
And then we had kids.
It all came back.
We were resorbed.
Flipping the pronouns in a poem
from "I" to "you" or "he" or "she"
is an easy way to suspend the gravity

of the facts of your mind
in favor of a less specific destiny.
But it is also dishonest.
Oedipus is the mirror image
of Abraham and Isaac.
They're synthesized in the monstrosity of children—
Frankenstein, *The Metamorphosis*, *Eraserhead*.
My kids aren't monsters,
but when we had them
the life the world draped over us
was the world's impossibility. Something
latent within the self
like an obscure definition of a familiar word
suddenly bursts into view
in the circuit between generations.
What I can never tell
is whether this force springs
from the roles that contain us
or is resistance to containment itself.
The latter would be more dignifying,
in its way, but I'm doubtful it's the case.
The circuit loops back.
It's as if I looked on your computer
and found you'd written this exact poem.
But not really. It's more like,
nevermind. The imagination is emptied
of fathers and sons,
of men, of concrete and abstraction,
now is just a line on a surface
curved into a letter

that is a refuge from other letters
that is pronounced by walking
back to its beginning
along a rosary of years.

CRYING DEAD LIGHTS

by the window hearing walkers
grating ease in their gait
talk of trips to South America
whether to hitchhike / their problems

lifetime at a stop sign
fall and rise of car sounds
waves
return to walls
old wreath
flakes of it everywhere
rainbow family painting

I remember calling from the airport to say
he didn't seem well to me
has anyone considered trauma counseling
or that was how he addressed himself
that part of himself that lived through it
and was unknown to me / inexpressible by him
to his satisfaction

movement in a bath
sighs and hands going up
I like the windows to be dirty
materiality of glass
very still
suppressing a cough

she blows her nose and pulls the drain

children taking over
their weird little voices / drastic need

reasoning with this cough
I need nothing
and neither do you
tap
wrap and drip

he walks in holding a box on his face
three long days everyone sick
a page every few hours
five years ago today
simple taps
they put the plate right in front of me
a little embarrassed it wasn't mine
I knew whose it was

Cairo, Outer Space
my feelings
Canada
read a million things
then come back
black bottles
make an exception
it's easier than you think
long lives
brommsa

forever of this

such often hair
big butterfly tattoo on everything
after I get it all waxed

hospitals when they don't give
nouns when we live together
he told me he lied to his therapist about me
that I'd said things
made it easier to get through it
has it always been interchangeable?
and yet he was the one who cheated
or sort of
making out

the real problem with the other one
was he was an asshole
I knew that when we got back together
I'm sure he's perfectly wonderful now
we all got older
owns a design store with his husband
like the one he worked at in his 20s
spent most of his paychecks there
such good taste
such a burden

sick as a dump truck
waiting on the second kid
angling for a middle name, Thunderbolt
bendable Jesus on the windowsill
between the carbon monoxide detector and the hand sanitizer

totems against probability
double meaning toenail color
"bond with whomever"

couldn't tell what I was seeing until it was him
we didn't know what it would be like
space space space space space
oh god that baby who died
melodrama in books / horror in life
like we said at work
good for the case / bad for humanity

the anxiety arrives in the form of questions
a scrum of reporters advancing upon the psyche
qualities of language other than sound
qualities of paint other than color
qualities of self other than experience
arrangement and buildup
two pink chairs, cardboard, and walking through
count everything between here and the wall
count the wall

gray and cold spring
buds in suspension after warmish head fakes
Elmer in the bathroom talking to his hands
"Let's back it up"
small plastic bugs in them
now flying through the house
Maggie and Harlan asleep or trying
exactly two weeks old

"You have a stinky diaper rawr"
early and no one outside
"I'm right here"
dog-walker in parka
the fortunate past
waiting under the lights
soliciting clones

new currents drift-stopping
gray manifesting as damp
cars everywhere now
the next letter is "j"
a secret service car
siblings
beige white blue brown
backlit greeting cards in the window
dark and ominous
forsythia in a turquoise vase
the secret service again
I used to think it was for Tom Perez
but Corey said his detail is FBI

that art
pacing and spacing
abstraction from the bottom
strangest when elemental
chunk overload
place one color in the mind and hold
there are times when Matisse
such as in the cut-outs

articulates despite himself
the difference between art and design
unremarkable pleasure
the constant risk of art
becoming culture

everyone up and swing a-trotting
four-footed duck drawing
larval squawk and lullaby electronica
Elmer licks the gobble plate
its inexplicable dog-turkey hybrid
we had to dig out all his old pacifiers
annoyed when I hold the baby
cartoonish waaaaah and arms up
we're waiting another month to start potty training
the next month I go back to work
he's a little over three

she's called me a prosecutor twice
any work for the sovereign
I try not to romanticize, but you spend a few years
banging your head against the wall of institutional reform
permit narratives to be rote
avoid provocative misprisions
loss cycles
apples at my feet
the car goes on idling
this midwife takes forever

abandonment aestheticism ambition

donation of intelligence and time
less than recommends itself
the discovery of prose in the '70s
as they killed the Equal Rights Amendment
in Title IX of the Civil Rights Act of 1964 it seems like
Congress believed that sex discrimination was *already*
prohibited by the Fourteenth Amendment
I can find things with a shape
whether to say it and how
all of the time there will ever be, cleaning
Hamlet-like consternation over the menu
I happen to be in the living room at the moment
all of his changes foreground life and his music
they drifted through the intersection oblivious to traffic
I don't like those pants on you
I don't know if she stooped over because of her age or the cold
I just needed to grow up

Elmer chatters rather than naps
beeps from the open fridge
zero dark mailman
morally ambiguous diaper
strains of class dominance in retail environmentalism
strains of ukulele
what is not prohibited is permitted
half the forsythia has changed
each person an audience
wood*pecker* is a bit of an understatement
garish and oblivious display
just finishing a game / zero to zero

the genre of markings upon surfaces
form barely filled out

NOON KNOWLEDGE

The point was more that
When we felt like this
This feeling that no
It would never feel natural
But what about possible
To experience eyes open
Somewhere close to acceptance
It became so important
For me the sense
Untiring sense
That what there should be
For any of us
Shouldn't be
Carried easily away
In the earliest particles of morning
But look at me
Keep looking
Heavy editing
May have removed all references to time
But the capacity of my scenes
I cry
Like who kills for us
Without our asking
Or constantly asking
Both fair inferences
From the things you hear
Endless screaming
Or an extended wail
That goes in and out

Across waves of static
As you turn your bike
Through its fiction
All the way to the yard
A day so long
Where's mine
A fifties haircut and the collected Cheever
A copy under each arm
Tawdry addictions to corduroy and mascara
Dedication to the slope
I would like
You to admit
My connections to the studios
Thirty or so identical creaks
And the lights decline
Behind red roofs and flat sky
White-gray with possible orange tint
Within which we are
Crowded in our passions
For tacit regard
The unexpected strings
Rising suddenly from the minute
Tilting of heads toward traffic
At the fifty-second convention
Held a thousand times a day
At the ends of this crosswalk
Everything else is exactly
Where we left it at lunch yesterday
Even me so stop staring
Stop it and go back to your hands

I'm not putting on a show up here
Not in the deliver-me-from-evil sense
For thine is not the kingdom
For thine is green
And yellow and red
Forever and ever
Lines pressed together into shapes
People risking their lives
For the artful mistake
That they'll outlast the snow
Believing themselves to be
Those we would most
Like to reach
But will never convince
We talk at their backs
Report it as meaning
Give up and move on
To whoever
Will be the next to go
And which side
Like we'd know
Wearing these light-up blindfolds
Tired of eyesight
To minimize contact
Put the setting at zero
And take it all down to nothing
Blue tarp snagged on fence
Blue warehouse behind
Windows all that matters
And the single orange curtain in one

Agile arrangements
Streets where you need them
And often where you don't
We're all leaving anyway
Unless we melt by comparison
Cheap candy that we are
Not in the genre of fuck
I would bestow
Upon their coiffed little balls
Hard as jobs
In the muscles of my face
We've taken a definite turn here
Who are these light bulbs
Cameras I should have known
It's never that bright
And yet dispositions
Seem to be real and filling
Most of the space in everyone's
Beliefs about their lot
The wellspring of half-hour religions
I've had a few
Half hours that is
The unicycle of intervals
I'm spending one now in fact
But as I do
I'm told I have a look
Let's assume that means my face
Though I would never discount
The intuitions of those who notice
The interiors of our souls

Or the spray of how-we're-bearing-upness
That in truth is so apparent
While you bob there in the puddle
Of this transseasonal week
I'm not a climate denier
But if it's all going to end
What does everybody have against now
That still wouldn't be the world
To worry so ambitiously
In casual pain
Not worthy of notice
Shameful in origin
As choices hydraulically constrict all mood options
Into narrow bands you strum
Chords it's important for you to believe
Are new and your own
Versions of auld lang syne
A song I've only heard in movies
A century in the making
All of that comes back to my mind
The place I need to be
A controversy vacuum
Sealed off from history
The most elegant privilege I could get
But what about being there
Am I there even partly
Homunculus on the Venn diagram
Turning my absent-minded gears
And water into other water
Or if I'm factually separate

Where would I be doing so
Among these fits of crying
I can't take really anything
Even gratitude impales me
Petals drop into the toilet
Rain fills the cupped hands of a statue
Person by person the CVS empties
The problem with noon knowledge
I wrote in my dream
Is that it's only noon
Which someone in my dream
Saw me write down
And told me I'd plagiarized
From the Bible no less
After I woke up
I googled the phrase noon knowledge
Which although not biblical
Actually seems to have some currency
In the English-speaking world
Used as the chatty name
For lunchtime information sessions
About retirement planning or blood-borne pathogens
In my dream someone made a point
Of showing me flowers under the noon sun
Their shadowlessness she said
Is what the Bible was referring to
As the problem with noon knowledge
So you see how
The present is inflected by noonness
Just a few days ago

After the line
Where would I be doing so
Above
I considered writing the line
Not within these natural spaces
And then copying and pasting the entire poem
After it so that everything would repeat
Read the poem that way one time
And tell me what you think
I wasn't sure it worked
But liked the effect and the idea
Maybe a new form
Transparent deliberate amateurish
Mined for concept a relationship to content
This is incidental at best
Arising less from history in general
Than from the specific history of poetry
Inapt dogmas the poverty of use
Fog slowing the lightening of the morning
Putting a blue filter on the day
Setting off the orange street lights
And well-lit interiors muting the buildings
Themselves a cave underneath
This landscape of weather
Among shipping containers in eccentric rows
That suggest little
Of the moods contained within them
The privacy of irrelevance eyes
And cameras making things
Darker by taking in their light time

Bleeding into clocks the movement
Of mercury in a thermometer
The residue it leaves as it falls

ACTUALLY PRESENT

the fabulous vanity of the present

something something something
something something something

the fabulous vanity of the present

THOSE FEELINGS OF COMPLETE DESPERATION

The room itself is about the size
of a public high school gym
in a smallish town an hour away
from the region's largest airport.
I'm standing at one end of it
squinting because of the sun
coming through a window
directly in front of me.
It is 7:45 a.m. on my black wristwatch.
I heard the door I came through lock behind me.
I have never been more in love.
The smell is unbearable.
Standing to my left
is a man muttering to himself.
A child is on the floor at his feet.
The child looks up at me and says,
"She's trying to ask you a question."
"What is the question?" I ask.
"I don't know. I can't understand her."
The sun has moved up in the sky.
My eyes are clear and closed.
The feeling of love courses through me
and pushes tears out of my face.
There's a relentless, swirling pressure
in my sinuses and hands
that seems part of a single, larger vector.
I am going to think all the way through this.
"What are you trying to keep to yourself?"
"Everything I can. It's a rolling landscape."

Should we perhaps communicate without punctuation
Yes I think that would be easier
Do you feel close to your loved ones
I feel embedded within them
The room fills with laughter.
Hundreds upon hundreds of laughters
going in a circle around the edges.
I am so curious to learn more about you.
Where did you grow up?
I'm sorry, I can't hear you.
Where did you grow up?

_____

Which parent were you closer to as a child?

_____

Which parent has the largest claim on you now?

_____

Could you describe a time when some part of your physical
body appeared to be someone else?

_____
_____
_____
_____
_____

Why have you pushed so many people out of your life?

_____

_____

_____

_____

_____

How do you account for the incongruity between the license you give yourself and the expectations you have of others?

_____

_____

_____

_____

_____

How, exactly, do you expect things to get better?

_____

_____

_____

_____

_____

I don't know how I missed it,
but the walls are the most intense
shade of green I have ever seen.
The sunlight yellowed the color before,
or maybe a glare, unacknowledged lobbyist

of the world, corrupted my impressions.
My face appears on the wall to my right.
Not my face at this moment
but at some other time.
I'm looking directly at me.
I don't remember making this recording,
if that's what it is,
maybe it's from the future.
The laughter stopped
when my face appeared on the wall.
Now all I can hear is a shushing sound,
not insistent, but soothing.
It's not coming from my face,
not the one on the wall, that face is now
speaking, but I hear the words
from my own mouth,
I'm talking uncontrollably,
saying, I think, what the wall is mouthing,
"Most of the time I'm either bored with myself or annoyed,
oscillating between those two depending on how angry I am.
Occasionally—*very* occasionally—I have that feeling
of satisfied self-regard, like you see on the faces of old people
at the end of commercials about retirement planning,
looking downward from a sun-drenched hillside,
as if to say something about how you could feel in the afterlife,
looking back and knowing you did good.
Like you left something meaningful and substantial.
Lately I've been trying to gauge the point after my death
at which the overwhelming feelings of regret begin to subside,
where I finally reach symmetry with my feelings

about the time before my birth.
That point seems to be the year 2100,
when I will surely be dead.
Everything between now and then is completely fraught,
but afterwards, like before my life, is someone else's homework."
Mirrors, ghosts, shadows, smoke, fog on English landscapes,
roses, rings, hearts, champagne, the tips of tiny snowflakes.
The room suddenly became very dark
except for a small, shapeless fleck of light
that fell directly upon the mouth of the person
muttering at my side. I looked at the mouth
and began to suspect that the muttering
carried no intention of making itself understood,
at least not in the conventional sense,
and that instead it was bestowing upon me
a physical address in the phone book of my experience
for the previously amorphous zones of my failures of meaning.
Then it occurred to me how fortunate
and unnerving that would be—   .
for all I could not understand to organize itself
into a single voice, just to my left.
A fog machine came on in front of me.
What is that particular smell?
A face, not my own, was projected into the fog.
The slow shifting of the fog gave the face
the appearance of movement,
or maybe the face was also moving.
The fog machine continued to fill the room
with smoke, and the billows, and thus the face,
came closer and closer to me,

its features changing so fluidly
that they were impossible to distinguish.
Before long the face had overtaken me,
and my body was inside it,
enveloped in smoke.

JEAN DUBUFFET JOHN WIENERS SHAWN KILLEBREW

To think of you
alone, scrolling through
paragraphs of streets
in winter syntax,
a motion all plastic
abrupt by
leaving him exactly
in his mortgaged
mess of consultations
the space thinks
its distances memorize.
Periodic island
on the occasional map
watching the tide.
You looked in my
time. You saw
what I said. To me
the meaning had parts
we couldn't speak
unless we took
everything else out
in public, in trouble
with the four of us
who wanted to find
the identity of our
unusual questions,
their odd phrasing
as mist, as fissures
along the ridge

of an apology
for levity without
legible grief.
Hopeless. Hopeless.
Red pickup truck.
Red pickup truck.
Red pickup truck.
Red pickup truck.
I see it.
You see it. You
don't see it.
Are you difficult
with me? Are you
different with me?
My doors, my hands,
loud no more in closing,
mute in fact,
but you left him
with language
stacked on love
or hmmm : : : : : : : : :
hum, passage of time,
bland faithfulness for
anything's sake
but your own,
impersonal rainbow
like art. To move
one's thinking
toward a coherent idea
that encompasses

all of the incipient
splinters tickling
your fingertips
as you run them along
the grain of this
feeling's horizon—
the problems of this
body, listed out
for miles so you
can read them
for the rest
of its life, all-
consuming distraction
from the true path
of the fan blade
through less and less
light smothering you
as he soberly
lowers the blinds
on his flirtation
with nearly genuine
concern, the most
compelling sound
a basic yes
left accidentally
in good old
breakfast, the mood
unwatchable by any
but the terminally
painted, pained by

being around him,
his unfortunate vigor
and perfect but
drained sensations
of living disasters
months in the unfurling.
Black hole, desire,
drawn to destruction
and its thorough
transformations, one
into more than one
and back
to zero,
one to zero to four,
zero to zero to two
to one, one and zero
to patterns alleged
in the wrinkles
of my dress,
accidental rhymes
in the arrangement
of my mind,
how far I am
from each other and you
despite my almost
complete control
over the shapes
I see when
the regular dimensions
no longer care

to understand whatever
I thought I
demanded of love.
So I pick up
the laundry,
the towels on the floor,
collect the cups
from the table
and dump the coffee
in the sky.
Ideas of blue
flash through
the blur my eyes
left of the drive
to Boulder
implanted by daytime
in a recollection
that strangely inhales
any emotive
tilts of mind
hitting the inside
of old now. Flat
sense. Quick limit.
To go entirely
too far with ideas,
I left the minute.
I didn't know anything.
I could guess like
any contestant on
so much adderall

the semicolons' come-
hither conjoining
of waves would appear
like a prelude
to the vows
I exchanged with my
body, that we run
parallel through time,
nod politely if
we happen to
stumble upon the other,
move on without
being too terribly
rude, resigned
to disappointments
we heap upon
each other and
of course our
impending divorce.
This could be it,
or this, or a television
of this. How the paintings
change in the mind,
is that television, too?
People through one
spot of glare?
Conglomerations of color
unable to escape
the cycle of regrets
into which they've

been embedded?
Mental tour busses?
Time has narrowed me
so I must try
new inflections
in styles more fortunate
in variation
that may, or so
I hope, dispute
the stasis into which
my body—pain
in duration—might
project a true
event of myself
even to me and perhaps
others, so that
I could know
something less obscure
than this antiquated
wardrobe of skin.
I go
to the parking lot
and attempt my
with beliefs,
my *or* beliefs,
my transposition practice,
one raised finger
circling between us
to bring our eyes
into shared consequence,

oh *please* already,
we were practically
birthed from the same
esophagus and *now*
you surrender all credit
for the disaster
of my company?
Clearly I'm feeling
as fuck of
something. And no and
no and no and *yes*,
okay Dabney Coleman,
you can have
all the emotions
in this shoebox,
the rest of us
will just sit here
eating crackers
like perfect pink sofas.
Departure is pure
grace if no one
sees, if no one
guesses that the basic
premise of daylight
is buried in an axiom
I blahly reject,
if no one mistakes me
for an expiration date
on bread claiming
authorship for its

baloney. I want a morning
off from this job
of persistence,
just a morning,
a pause in being
to step back
a pace or two,
get the scale
with my pencil
and sign my name
in the corner
with natural flourish,
hearts and flowers
and infinite vowels
spoken instantly
as a briefly audible
sigh, like breath
drawn to the side
and bumping into
a creaky door,
so much for secrets.
Mine is failed
speech therapy,
a vintage "s"
as yet untamed
by these liars
in lilting hair
with respectability
chiseled into their
brains for slow

submission to
futures I'm neither
called nor invited
to the exacting
pronunciation of.
Circle back,
renew the predicate,
renew the concept
of predicate by
brushing off a helipad
for its descent
among other impressions
left embryonic
by distraction's
parasitic flirtations
with nowness,
itself an infection
of the mind's
belief in mind,
a habitat for laughter,
a habit of breathing
backwards, sleeping
in reverse, big jolly
hellos screamed
underwater with veins
popping out
of your eyeballs,
the catalog section
of winter neighborhood
filling the window

with page after page
of snow, of
studious examination
of left blinker,
left blinker,
commuters at angles,
left blinker,
left blinker,
left blinker,
the first conversation,
left blinker,
left blinker,
ever between boxes,
left blinker,
left blinker,
left blinker,
left blinker.

ANYONE'S TWO MINUTES

The moon is empty,
whatever else may be happening
in the change of setting.
He removes his hand
from the inner pocket of his blazer,
and it is empty.
Her hand finds its way
from her hip to his
and then across his back,
flat and moving upward
until her fingers hook
just over his collar
and tug just barely.
"I just thought," she continued,
"we could extend to each thought
the courtesy of completing it."
The small crowd
that had coagulated around her
broke into laughter. The ceiling caved right in.
Pure imitation is only possible
in the cult of authenticity,
for these are the flowers of our youth,
the cant of glorious magmas
instantiated in molecular puzzles
of personally offending highwire commentary
delivered in drollest New England chowder.
Exhale of concept.
The future of the worker is closing its doors.
It's fine with me if nothing happens.

I expect some feelings of disappointment,
but they won't encompass us,
not with so many dots to fill in
and the regular accomplishing of sentences
in the high-spirited yellow living room,
steam of small dishes
against the cold weather,
children's desperation, a loosening
of screens, a face at the window
receding. The darkness,
as they say, abounds within us.
He choked to death on his own joke.
The dogs had some kind of dispute.
Choose a glass from this tray and wait.
She smiled from the corner of the stadium.
I borrowed this car from a sick neighbor.
The signs insist all they like.
I think we know better.
No one delivers a punch like me.
I can't even feel my hands.
It's been ages since I thought of this.
Please help.
We're desperate for your love.
Revise at will and send on.
I can't wait to hear what you think.
Then I consider explaining to him just how awful he is to me.
I lost all interest in ever saying anything.
I just sat there and took it.
I don't expect to stay much longer.
I just don't see how I could.

TO LITERALLY YOU

Who do you know here, exactly? Desire
to be temporary
as an era
retreating as it advances
in massive blobs
obscuring its movement,
sheets of earliness trailing onto the floor
or what we think the nineties represents,
like as an artwork,
a ground or a sky, ordinary crime.
No one twenty years ago,
no one now.
A grass blade arcs over another
in the music of space
with so little known about anything,
much less each other,
and, to be clear,
I have the least hope in myself,
I'm all out there
in the promising distance
where there seem to be plenty of adults,
though too many explanations
given the scarcity
of bona fide consequences.
We share that blame
like a last name
among those of no relation,
a default setting
requiring constant readjustment.

What can one do
but step carefully
around the perverse reveries
of the snowmen who have taken over
this once-peaceful neighborhood of animals?
Over in the shadows
of their strained retorts,
I pronounce the marriage
of prohibition and permission
and descend the lunar staircase
through the seven houses of the future zodiac:
Wrinkle of Lip,
Shoulder Blade,
Lungs,
Elbow Skin,
Undifferentiated Gonad,
Hamstring,
and Center Toenail.

*****

Have you ever noticed
that a lot of people are away on vacation?
Even this rock is sinking deeper into the sunshine
that's been the glossary of my personality
unfolding a series of overlaid remarks
meant to distract my listeners
from the crisis of pure lies
that permits me to speak at all.
Speak? That hardly seems feasible

in the crosshairs of a microscope
where each particle of meaning
is far too much as it seems
for anything like sympathy
to cloud the elegant formulas
by which the extent of my love
is divided by its failures.
Profligate failure! Of memory descending,
the shirt I unbutton, religious shadows
latched to morning commuters,
the line you've drawn
through the water
that surrounds the humble farmhouse
where Ma and Pa
are moving the dishes to a higher shelf
and praying that this weeklong storm
will cease its endless threat
of making their children
vulnerable to the charms
of mysterious strangers on horseback
murmuring promises of boundless fortunes
to be made by those
willing only to believe.
Everything had been so simple,
their days had been like keys on a piano
all tuned to play the same note.
Why didn't they just give the man
his seven dollars and leave?
It's too late now, night is upon them,
the rain is getting colder, bigger.

A fog has fallen.
They watch in trepidation
as the first rivulets
spring through the doorjamb.

*****

I've loved you without delay,
all immediacy and concrete,
life stopped entirely
then lurching on impossibly
through jobs and disinterest,
I thought that, too,
I remember now,
we were leaving together,
we had the same perspective,
vectors of speech
that failed the seductive majesty of image
but manifested in sound
stupid repetitive time,
coworkers who said every word
that came out of their mouths
and ate all the horseshit
they could stand.
It's something, isn't it,
to be so amenable?
By the time they say jump,
you are already
in the water.
You feel it going into your ears,

your nose, even draining
through your eyelids
into your skull
and surrounding your brain,
which feels buoyant and detached.
You close your eyes
to stop the water from coming in,
but then new eyes sprout up
directly on the outside of your brain
and open, stingingly, into the darkness.
You sense them adjusting
to the light and salinity,
it's a strange feeling
that they can't see anything
and presumably never will,
and yet there they are, without question,
open and ready.

*****

Oh, people. Oh . . . people.
The ridiculous ocean of your specificity.
The ridiculous ocean of *my* specificity.
The ridiculous ocean of YOUR specificity!
The ridiculous ocean of *MY* specificity!!!
Meanwhile, the small robotic dog
continues his journey
across the yellow square.
Whose time is this to waste?
Anyone's, unperturbed but distraught,

pursued through scary dimensions
in hopes of insight, like in sci-fi,
but left instead with an empty week,
empty of nameless verbs
sweating through a thick powder application,
beads of it popping out across the cheek
like a translucent rash,
like water jelly spread over skin toast,
like tiny volcanic islands forming out of glass,
like liquid pathos,
like flags of surrender to the heat,
like anxiety made flesh,
and I'm so sorry these days are so long
and that we spend so much of them
roaring pleasantries
through the thick walls
that separate my luminous hopes
from your own.
Do you get the feeling
that we will never actually meet?
And that never meeting
is the danger of our love?
Our love is dangerous,
cast in downward glances
and tepid papers
flung into the air.
It leaves me giggling and terrified
of what you'll say
and what I know you can't.

WHAT I TOOK TO BE RESIGNATION

"I couldn't see the video," she said,
"because everyone was crowded around,
and it was such a small screen."

And after a period of sustained reflection
I abandoned the bits of mirror
I spent so many years holding
in the margins of my eye,
but then the window, bent,
distended the impending intuition,
that woeful moment
when the owl spoke
but not to me. What a lump
I made of those noodles.
And I couldn't understand
how the seventies never got
any farther away,
they always seemed to be
just a few ideas back,
imitating our cadences with a slight
exaggeration, as in: I love you,
I have always loved you!
Who among me would rather
call down some bored spirit?
The vernacular keeps its own time,
ossifying the maudlin
pastels I cannot, any longer,
stand my self outfitted without

but also cannot manage
to fit this unconscious stranger
within. How would he *rather* wake up?
Sun obliterating trees,
some new mailman getting familiar
with the cracks in his cheap blinds,
his arm wrist-deep in a bowl
of longing, *that shirt! those syllables!*?
We could all improve our elocution.
My manner mistakes (mistaken?)
for a person very much like myself,
one who challenges my sense
of complicity with the uniqueness myth
one tells and is told
with each passage of the comb
through the narrative complexities
attending such juicy impersonations
as one might accomplish
on the never-ending flight to prison,
the prison of each face meeting one's own,
especially one's own
in those moments of purest bisexuality.
My glasses! You found them!
Finally I can read the numbers
I've been chiseling into the doorway
of this dream. Dear me I hope
it doesn't turn out to be French,
those funny *ones*. But that's not *real*
imagination, not like torching a rented minivan
or commuting with an ex.

That's right, Mom and Dad,
I can make my *own* anxiety!
A small capsule of green letters later
and just watch the pronouns converge
into the feeling of shhhhhhhhhhhhhhhhhhh,
ommmmmmmm in fizzy water,
credit card melting short story,
a caption that reads "not for rent,
not for sale, only to be seen,"
the purest investment, purely extraneous,
the culture's most harmless
little bite of your art:
misdirection in satin,
a stain on the hem.
It took me years to find this blouse,
and now I just have it.
I don't like to talk about it.
I wouldn't know how.
That's his real selling point—
angles of rebuff in the lonely repartee
he wears to those appointments
at hesitation weekend, the gathered drunks
inching closer each time
he takes a long pull on his eyelids
and grows nostalgic along that same, tired vector,
like his memories obey the laws of physics
and bend toward the heaviest object,
a mind of clear video.
These last few days
have circled around me

like graphics, or is that not
what they're called anymore,
or a concept like childhood
that's useless because no two
are even remotely alike.
Of course we've made certain promises
that there is no one in this world
we so much want to see,
no one more fitting for this leap
into the arms of more words
washed out under the klieg lights
and turned three-quarters away,
glancing back with chins on their shoulders,
eyes navigating the unsteady sojourn
down their patrician noses.
I think what we're looking for here is
"unapproachable." Years pass and looks fade,
and eventually no one remembers
what had seemed indelible,
at least to me, the former resident,
how I emerged from the fog
onto an empty moon
without a clue how I got there
but determined nevertheless to revise
provocation into beads of sound
that could be arranged and re-arranged
without losing the life-giving qualities
that first woke me up, drenched in tears,
gripping the surface of time
and recognizing what had until then

been misspelled in my mind,
that the present filters an extravagant past
into a future of endless scarcity.
But you know how easy it is
to overplay a clarity
into muteness. When I left town,
I left without my keys.
That skinny day!
How a disorienting openness in the clouds
inspired your hand so casually
to reach from the back seat
to brush confetti from my hair!
How that kid next to his mailbox
slowly unfolded a piece of paper!
I felt too delicate for such intimacy.
I wanted to be on the phone.
I wanted to run my fingers through the wires
and rewrite the Easter scene from *Steel Magnolias*.
But it wasn't to be mine.
I always dive into numbers
when I only know the first few names
and show up a day early for graduation.
It circles around and around.
I could walk off the set
or make cheese to waste yards and daylight,
as if a few weeks is all I really need
to pull this whole thing together.
But deep down I know
the real problem is the script.
Gullible as I surely am,

I just can't re-imagine anymore,
and I have that promiscuous skin
that absorbs any passing radiation
or under-breath commentary
from the walnut gallery.
Such a delicate lollipop,
and so tired! But that's what
this recurring car accident is—
a car accident and a car accident
and a car accident and a car accident.
And me, every time,
holding the same suitcase
full of the same promises,
less and less able to feign shock,
which, to be frank, makes me most suspicious
of myself. What else is culpability
if not a lack of surprise?
And let's not forget that the dial
goes all the way around—
you saw the TV in the street,
you know what makes a star.
Trees arced over the road
drop leaf shadows through bright glare,
disorganizing the ground
like a spilled puzzle.
Past happiness. To light rain.
My gender declensions. Small evocations,
blessedly nonspecific in convergence,
anyone at a moment's notice
but not in the real life of months,

email, banging out left turns—
something much slower
and observable, an empty airport.
So methodical with my makeup,
so quiet in the evacuation.
Personally I hope these tunnels
never end. I know that's not
a popular sentiment, but I'm not here
that way, this isn't my noun
to fish out of the sensation.
It could probably be yours
if you want it, if you like
meandering little dots of and
bottlenecking at random intersections
strafing today's map of human data,
of which this is a gif.
Like an angelic customer
looped steadily into violation
or the practice of synthetic time,
I ask the question of novelty
with each in-going breath
and each exhale is an answer.
Good morning said the graffiti.
Good morning replied the wall.
May we gerrymander a mood together
around these artifacts of feeling.
I've wanted them like I've wanted you,
conspicuously so I can stop talking
and seeing might be plenty
and plentiful. But eyes can never

be depended upon to be
just, isn't that the problem?
No, it's not. I'm suffused with agency,
that's the problem. And if I don't like it,
I can just take this elevator built for one
all the way up to the bathroom and *cry!*
Like a real dinosaur.
Peace of the circumscribed—
reasons I rotate within—
social money and lilt—
ten-speed toleration street—
anxiety as immediacy—the phone
of my body on vibrate—
walking on toenails—to make
nothing from something—to Maryland
repose. My inclination is to leave
through the passing door on wheels
before anyone notices the question
on their hands or the drinks I'm siphoning
from the other party woven into this one,
fewer but heightened, unnoticed
by the bilious mouth-heads
this costume community seems to summon
like spam, thankfully planning their permanent removal.
Step into the red dot and wait.
There. Now you can go.
But the door is gone!
Trying not to draw attention,
I bend down and reach into my sock
for the zipper I recently installed

above my heel, but I can't find it. Fine.
I prefer swimming anyway,
and now I'm a pool. But *then*
you tell me you don't even *like*
gymnastics. Can you handle another rainout?
Do you want these teeth in writing?
Such a weird little edit won't mollify the sick chairs
leaning deeper into their pathologies
of complete understanding, their failures
to recognize what remains unfinished within them
and the contagious distortions
of so much ill-gotten sense-making.
Their astonishment is scheduled for another seance
with an unnoticed medium through which
seamless meaning manifests as personality,
a coherence of affect masking schools of traffic
I personally find the more charming suggestion
of what is actually not merely invisible
but unseeable. They have the slippage of synonyms,
different then same then different again,
but differently, like a street you lived on years ago,
or was it another? Sometimes all one has
is the mysticism of the unplaceable familiar,
which itself amounts to faith in connectedness
scored with faith's longing for need.
To hold that out as the truest line
between fantasies of self and other—
I'm not without admiration.
But apparently I see so much more to be gained
from my glistening collection of tuxedoed clouds

that find me hopelessly naive
with my mispronounced pauses and aporias.
You learn so much by faking your way
through enough of the early exams
to earn the pink heartache
that opens before you like a birth
that is also a path through your own body
to its imperious destination, disappearance
from any idea, only fact and presence,
a feeling always just over the cusp
of this one or stumbled upon accidentally
like an acquaintance you'd be happy
to find one day in a pocket of music
formed by a snag in the current
of rushing sensations and the language
that impels them, not fully your own.
I learned along the stairstep of friendship
to see my pasta in the barrage of how-dos
pummeling my welcoming little wink
during the holdout of the introductory rate.
I learned to see the ones for me.
Usually there weren't any, never
more than one or two, never enough
that I could drop the paper accent and be
everything this beached starfish can imagine.
So maybe I never should have taken that CPA exam,
or maybe I'm happy *not* to be licking dew
off the handlebars of some wounded muppet revival.
When I was ten or eleven I lay down in leaves
I'd raked into a pile in the front yard

and stayed there for *hours*—
my finest approximation so far.
Not designed for comfort, this unshakeable cover.
Does that elevate my fidgeting to a kind of realism,
or is that acquisitive thinking? I'm not an owner
or don't want to be, not a Virginia statute
slowing rotation that is really a spiral
as all circles are in time, across time,
within, submersion, suffocation, breathlessness,
the last new thing and without antecedent,
like thought, of me but outside me, to the side,
isn't that why we do it, think, to branch off
from the emulsion or pretend to, to be
over *there*, regarding, instead of running
too fast out of space between flowers
or filling every fall in the cadence
with mono compositions of static sight,
chips of inhumanity so small
that even their existence could be debated
by the willfully destructive and unaccountable.
At the time we pass them over
along with all the other plans
we don't know we're making
for the longest day of our lives
to be captured in its entirety on film
by a purple-eyed photographer of language
trapped by his own premises
in a fur-lined exposition of the soul
as the ablation of personhood by time.
"My point," you replied, "is that

regardless of the truth of our understandings
about biological differences between the sexes
our urge to differentiate is pathological."
Or maybe I misheard. Recently
I was reminded how easily an adverb
can overwhelm its tormentor
on the loop of assemblage
this world so relentlessly
resembles. Never a less complicated ensemble
for my European creditors,
never a less expensive politics,
never an art without cursives,
never a word without bloating.
Glottal escapes *are* escapes:
you can leave through them
as a silence clarifies the sound
and its necessity as a place of arrival,
a thisness beside which I will forever
be a disappointment. It doesn't matter
if I tried, or *what*, or how *hard* I tried—
it doesn't matter when the voice I have is unhearing.
Culture of genes notwithstanding!
An impossible object, a collation of pure repetitions
appearing in the too rarely protested
cuts abridging the vista
for the sake of its conceptualization—
that's knowledge, bestowed by grace,
inaccessible otherwise, inaccessible to me,
visible shipments invisibly carried.
A baleful hum begins, rises, and moves,

its turns sketching the tear's path
falling across a landscape of sleep, dividing
wakefulness from its programming, style
from experience, the hidden reality
from the acknowledged fantasy
of ordinary words, ordinal moments
lined up down a morning
that blossom into story
almost convincingly, closely enough
most of the time, though we have those days
when nearby talk turns out to be a movie
and the place we were looking for
another life.

ACKNOWLEDGMENTS

Endless gratitude to Joshua Edwards, Lynn Xu, Robyn Schiff, and Nick Twemlow, the brilliant editors of Canarium Books.

Thank you Maggie Jackson, Travis Nichols, Monica Fambrough, and Katie Geha for reading these and other poems and talking to me about them.

Thank you to the editors of *Oversound*, *Folder*, and *The Equalizer*, where some of these poems previously appeared, sometimes in a slightly different form.

Paul Killebrew was born in 1978 in Nashville, Tennessee. His other books of poetry are *Flowers* and *Ethical Consciousness*, both published by Canarium Books. He currently resides in Maryland with his family.